Hidden World

WELDON OWEN PTY LTD

Chairman: John Owen
Publisher: Sheena Coupe
Associate Publisher: Lynn Humphries
Managing Editor: Helen Bateman
Design Concept: Sue Rawkins
Senior Designer: Kylie Mulquin
Production Manager: Caroline Webber
Production Assistant: Kylie Lawson

Text: Sharon Dalgleish
Consultant: Craig Sowden, Curator, Sydney Aquarium
U.S. Editors: Laura Cavaluzzo and Rebecca McEwen

04 03 02 01 00 99
10 9 8 7 6 5 4 3 2 1

Published in the United States by
Shortland Publications, Inc.
P.O. Box 6195
Denver, CO 80206-0195

Printed in Australia.
ISBN: 0-7699-0492-0

CONTENTS

EARLY EXPLORERS

In 1872, a group of scientists set out from England on a four-year voyage to study the world's oceans. They took rock and mud samples and recorded temperatures and currents. Their ship, the HMS *Challenger*, had laboratories so the scientists could examine the plants and animals they scooped up from the seafloor. Their findings filled 50 books—but the study of the oceans had only just begun.

STRANGE BUT TRUE

The legend of Atlantis tells of an island city, with temples of gold and silver, which disappeared into the sea. People wonder if a real Atlantis ever existed.

A HIDDEN WORLD

Continental Shelf
The edge of a continent is covered by shallow water and may once have been dry land.

What if you could suck away all the water in the world's oceans? You would see huge mountains, deep valleys, and flat plains, just like on dry land. A shallow shelf extends into the sea and then the seafloor plunges into the ocean depths. Scientists use special ships and equipment to piece together a picture of the deep-sea landscape. They are learning more about this hidden underwater world with the help of rock samples, computers, and maps of the seabed.

Continental Slope
The land near the coast gently slopes to form the side of an ocean basin.

Seamounts
These underwater mountains form islands if they rise above the surface of the water.

GLORIA
This is a mapping instrument attached to a ship by a cable. It sends waves of sound down to the seafloor and records the echoes.

Abyssal Plains
These are the flattest places on Earth.

Oceanic Ridge
A ridge is formed when new matter wells up from inside the Earth.

Oceanic Trench
Long, narrow valleys can be deeper than the height of the highest mountain on land.

BY THE SEA

Many creatures have
adapted to life at the sea's
shores. Some of these creatures
have hard shells that protect
them from birds, the hot sun, and
pounding waves. Others shelter among coral
or seaweed, or under rocks. Some appear only
to catch their prey, and then they
burrow into the sand and disappear.

Garibaldi
These fish make
their homes in
gaps in rocks.

Acorn Barnacles
These feed only when the tide comes in.

Periwinkles
These snails can be found just below the waves on rocky shores.

Kelp
This provides food and shelter for many sea creatures.

Sea Urchins
Some sea urchins have a painful venom.

LIFE IN A TIDE POOL

Each day, rocky shores flood with water as the tide comes in. When the tide goes out again, the rocky shores are exposed to the sun and air. The creatures that live in tide pools have to survive this daily wet and dry cycle. When the

MAKE YOUR OWN TIDE POOL VIEWER

What you need
- 1 empty milk carton (washed)
- scissors
- plastic food wrap
- rubber band

1 Cut off the top and bottom of a milk carton.

2 Cover one end with plastic wrap and secure it with a rubber band.

3 Tilt the viewer as you put it in the water so you get a good view.

Step three

Steps one and two

Hermit Crab
These crabs live in the old shells of other creatures.

tide comes in, the rocky shore comes alive with the activity of creatures feeding. Sea stars, or starfish, turn their stomach inside out to swallow their prey. Sea anemones sting their prey with waving tentacles. Mussels filter tiny bits of food from the rising water.

Octopus
Small octopuses are common—but very shy! They are not often seen by people.

Mussels
Mussels often grow in clumps.

Anemone
A sea anemone looks like a plant, but it's actually an animal.

Crab
Many small crabs live in tide pools.

Sea Star
Sea stars move slowly on hundreds of tiny feet.

MOTHER AND CHILD

Humpback whales push their
newborn calves to the surface
for their first breath. A calf is
about one-third the length of
its mother when it is born.

SHALLOW WATERS

The richest parts of the ocean are the coastal seas that
are near the edges of continents—the continental shelves.
These shallow waters teem with sea life. Tiny plants and
animals called plankton drift near the surface and can
make the water look very green. Plankton is an important
part of the ocean food chain. Herring eat plankton by
filtering it from the water, then fast-swimming fish feed
on the schools of herring.

DID YOU KNOW?

Not all crabs walk sideways. You can tell which way a crab will walk by looking at its shell. If the shell is longer than it is wide, the crab will generally walk forward.

FANTASTIC JOURNEYS

Some underwater creatures make journeys of thousands of miles to find warmer seas, more food, or a safe place to breed and raise their young. These journeys are called migrations. Whales mate and give birth in warm seas, but they migrate to polar seas to find the huge amounts of food they need. Sea turtles swim long distances to lay their eggs on the same beach where they themselves were hatched.

HOW FAR DO THEY GO?
These are the average distances traveled by these underwater creatures in their regular migrations.

green turtle
1,860 miles (3,000 km)

king crab
62 miles (100 km)

white bass fish
1 ¼ miles (2 km)

bluefin tuna
1,675 miles (2,700 km)

MYSTERIES OF MIGRATION

How do sea turtles find their way over open ocean to reach their special nesting sites? No one knows—not even scientists!

sockeye salmon
2,170 miles (3,500 km)

humpback whale
4,340 miles (7,000 km)

eel larva
1,860 miles (3,000 km)

northern fur seal
3,100 miles (5,000 km)

LIFE CYCLE OF A TURTLE

1. On the Beach
The female hauls herself slowly onto the sand and climbs the beach to look for a good spot to dig her nest.

2. Buried Safely
She digs a hole about 2 feet (½ meter) deep. She lays about 100 eggs in the hole, covers them with sand, and returns to the sea.

3. Race to the Sea
The Sun's heat warms the eggs until they hatch, and the baby turtles make a dash for the sea. Most do not survive.

Female green turtles leave their feeding grounds usually every two years to swim the enormous distance to their nesting sites. They make the journey alone—but once they reach the right beach, there could be thousands of turtles nesting at the same time. Millions of eggs are laid before the adults return to the sea. Hatching is a dangerous time for the baby turtles, as they have to rush to the sea to escape hungry crabs and birds. In the sea, sharks and other fish wait to eat them. Less than 1 in 100 will live to become an adult.

4. The Open Ocean
The young turtle finds its way to the feeding areas. Males will never again leave the sea. Females leave only to return to the same beach to lay their own eggs.

UPPER LEVEL
1. cod
2. green turtle
3. mackerel
4. flying fish
5. Portuguese man-of-war
6. dolphin
7. bluefin tuna
8. prawn
9. sperm whale
10. squid
11. shark
12. swordfish

MIDDLE LEVEL
13. hatchet fish
14. dragonfish
15. lanternfish
16. viperfish
17. octopus

BOTTOM LEVEL
18. gulper eel
19. anglerfish
20. deep-sea eel
21. bivalve
22. anglerfish
23. whalefish
24. cusk eel
25. rattail
26. brittlestar
27. crinoid
28. short-armed sea star
29. glass sponge
30. tripod fish
31. lamp shell

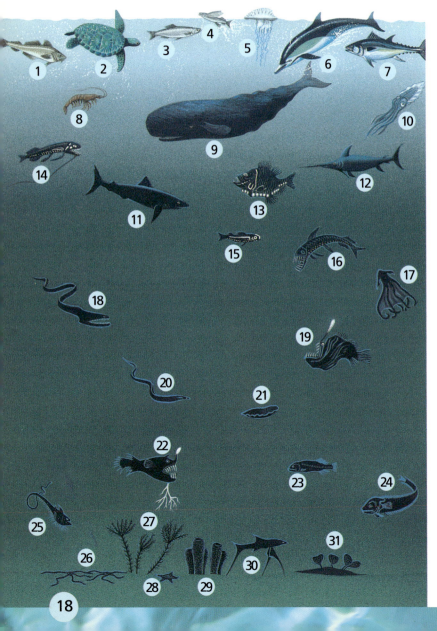

FROM TOP TO BOTTOM

Imagine that the ocean is a tall building. Sunlight can reach only the top floor, so this is where all the plants grow and where most of the food is. The creatures that live on the top floor eat as much food as they want, and the scraps they leave behind drop down to the floors below. As the food sinks down, all the creatures on the way down eat what they want. By the time the food reaches the bottom floor, there's not much left! That's why the creatures that live on the dark bottom swim slowly or simply drift around. They are saving their energy while they wait for food.

DID YOU KNOW?

When a female black dragonfish is young, it has eyes on long stalks. As the fish grows, the stalks are absorbed. By the time it is an adult, its eyes are in its head.

Smoke
Hot water and black smoke
rich in sulphur gush out of
vents in the seafloor.
Deep-sea creatures use the
sulphur to make their food.

Tube Worms
Tube worms grow in
clusters around the vent.
They absorb bacteria
through their skin.

Lava
Lava heats the
water to more
than 1,100° F
(600° C).

Clams
Giant clams filter
tiny bits of food
from the water.

Cold Water
Cold water seeps down
through the seafloor.

OASIS IN THE DEEP

The ocean floor is cold, dark, and still. There is no sunlight, no waves, and very little food. Cracks in the ocean ridge form vents like chimneys that gush hot water into the icy blackness. Communities of deep-sea creatures cluster around these vents. Tube worms, which have red plumes for breathing, grow up to 3 feet (1 meter) in length. Giant clams grow beside the vents. Strange fish swim in the warm water. The vent community is like an oasis in the deep-sea desert.

Fish
Scientists know very little about the fish that live in the deep sea on the edges of vent communities.

Crabs
Crabs scavenge for food.

EXPLORING THE DEPTHS

For hundreds of years, people have struggled to explore the ocean depths, using metal helmets, diving suits, and diving bells. Yet only a small part of the ocean has been explored. A scuba diver can safely dive to 165 feet (50 m). The deepest parts of the ocean may be 7 miles (11 km) below the surface! These depths can be reached only by small submarines called submersibles. As technology improves, we will discover more about this watery frontier.

HOW DEEP CAN THEY GO?

1. Conshelf 1965—330 ft. (100 m)
2. Tuna—650 ft. (200 m)
3. Diving Saucer 1959—1,350 ft. (412 m)
4. JIM suit—1,440 ft. (439 m)
5. Johnson Sea-Link—1,950 ft. (600 m)
6. Nuclear submarine—2,300 ft. (700 m)
7. Giant squid—3,300 ft. (1,000 m)
8. Dolphin submarine 1988—5,000 ft. (1,525 m)
9. Bathysphere 1934—3,028 ft. (923 m)
10. Deep Sea Rescue Vessel 1988—5,000 ft. (1,525 m)
11. Cyana 1975—9,800 ft. (3,000 m)
12. Turtle—10,000 ft. (3,050 m)
13. Alvin—13,000 ft. (4,000 m)
14. Sea Cliff 1988—20,000 ft. (6,100 m)
15. Deep Tow—20,000 ft. (6,100 m)
16. Trieste 1960—35,800 ft. (10,910 m)

DID YOU KNOW?

Jason is a remote-controlled camera robot. The crew of the submersible *Alvin* used it to explore the wreck of the *Titanic* on the ocean floor.

helicopter pad

drill pipes

lifeboat

satellite dishes

STRANGE BUT TRUE

Oil is a fossil fuel, formed from plants and animals that died millions of years ago. When the sand they were buried in turned to rock, the heat and pressure turned the plant and animal remains into drops of oil.

revolving crane

flare

well heads

processing
equipment

DRILLING FOR OIL

An oil platform is like a huge hotel in the middle of the ocean. Hundreds of workers live on the platform, staying there for weeks at a time. A platform is built from steel and concrete and is pinned to the sea floor with a framework of cables and pipes. It can stay in position for 25 years, and can pump millions of barrels of oil from the rocks below the seabed. It takes thousands of years for oil to develop, so there is a limited amount of it in the world. When it is all gone we will have to use other forms of energy.

mast

staging bay

main lab

AN OCEAN LAB

The ocean covers more than two-thirds of the Earth's surface. Research ships make it possible to explore some of this huge area. The first research ship set sail in 1872. Today, scientists study currents, the structure of the ocean floor, the effects of burning fossil fuels, and how the oceans interact with the atmosphere. Research ships often have a crew of about 20 to run the ship, plus 30 scientists working in well-equipped laboratories. They can even stay in touch with home by satellite communication.

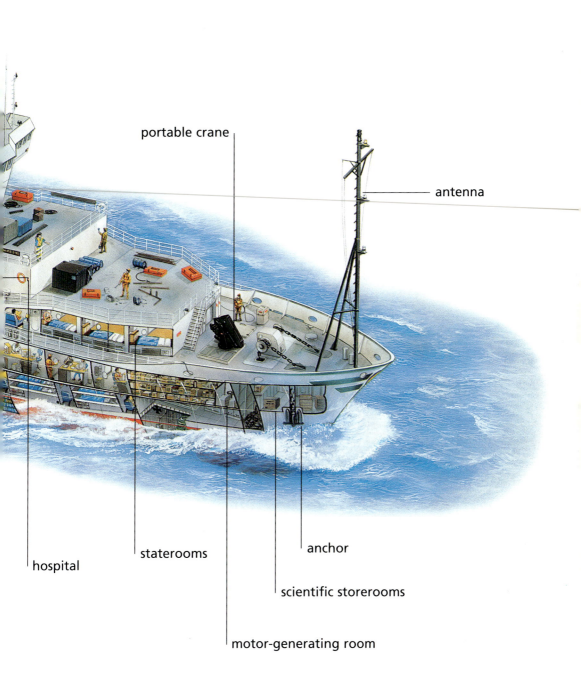

portable crane

antenna

hospital

staterooms

anchor

scientific storerooms

motor-generating room

CONSERVING THE OCEANS

We need the vast resources of the ocean for food, fuel, and energy. How can we keep them from being used up completely? Many nations have signed agreements to limit harmful fishing activities. In some areas, fish farms have been set up to boost numbers of certain types of fish. Marine parks have been created to protect endangered species and environments. There is still much to do—but we can all help by reducing the amount of pollution that reaches the ocean.

STRANGE BUT TRUE

The crown-of-thorns sea star has caused great damage to coral reefs during the last 20 years. It stays hidden during the day, then at night it feeds on the coral, leaving behind nothing but a skeleton. Tritons are natural predators of the crown-of-thorns sea star.

triton

crown-of-thorns sea star

African Tilapia
These fish are popular on fish farms.

Lobsters
These need to be conserved so their numbers stay high.

Tuna
Tuna fishing is restricted so tuna numbers can grow.

Whales
A ban on whaling has helped whale numbers grow.

Salmon
Polluted rivers destroy their breeding grounds.

Cod
Some fishing areas are damaged and have to be closed.

Sardines
Over-fishing has led to a drop in numbers.

Pollution
Enclosed seas are even more at risk from pollution.

GLOSSARY

atmosphere The thin layer of gases that surrounds planets such as the Earth.

currents Bodies of water that move continuously in a certain direction.

desert An area that receives little or no moisture during the year.

diving bell A bell-shaped container that receives air through a hose and is designed to take people deep under water.

fossil fuel A fuel such as oil, coal, and natural gas that has formed from plant or animal remains deep within the Earth.

lava Super-heated, liquid rock that flows up through the Earth's crust and out of volcanic vents.

migration The journeys animals make from one habitat or climate to another at specific times of the year.

oasis An area in a desert that has enough water for plants to grow.

plankton Groups of tiny plants and animals that live and float together through bodies of water.

tides The alternating rise and fall of large bodies of water caused by the gravitational pull of the Moon and Sun on the Earth.

vents Openings in the Earth's crust that allow built-up gases and heat to escape into the water or air.

INDEX

Credits and Notes

Picture and Illustration Credits

[t=top, b=bottom, l=left, r=right, c=center, F=front, B=back, C=cover, bg=background]

Jim Chan 10bl. **Corel Corporation** 13bc, 30br. **Simone End** 28br, BC. **Christer Eriksson** 8–9c. **Jon Gittoes** 10–11rc, 18c, 20–21c. **Mike Gorman** 29c. **Richard Hook/Bernard Thornton Artists UK** 4–5c. **David Kirshner** 19b, FCc. **Frank Knight** 14–15b, 16–17c, 31tl. **Alex Lavroff** 1c, 22bc. **PhotoEssentials** 4–32 borders, Cbg. **The Photo Library** 4b. **Oliver Rennert** 6–7rc, 23c. **Trevor Ruth** 15tr, FCtr. **Rod Scott** 12–13tc, FCb. **Stephen Seymour/Bernard Thornton Artists UK** 2b, 24b, 24–25c, 26–27c.

Acknowledgements

Weldon Owen would like to thank the following people for their assistance in the production of this book: Jocelyne Best, Peta Gorman, Tracey Jackson, Andrew Kelly, Sarah Mattern, Emily Wood.